THE LIFE OF CHARLEMAGNE

THE LIFE OF
CHARLEMAGNE

by

EINHARD

With a Foreword by Sidney Painter

ANN ARBOR PAPERBACKS
The University of Michigan Press

Seventh printing 1967
First edition as an Ann Arbor Paperback 1960
All rights reserved
Foreword copyright © by The University of Michigan 1960
Published in the United States of America by
The University of Michigan Press and simultaneously
in Rexdale, Canada, by Ambassador Books Limited
Translated from the *Monumenta Germaniae,* with Notes
and a Map, by Samuel Epes Turner
Manufactured in the United States of America

FOREWORD

by Sidney Painter

Charlemagne or Charles the Great who is counted as Charles I in the conventional lists of kings of France was one of the truly imposing figures of history. At the height of his power he ruled all the Christian lands of Western Europe except the British Isles and southern Italy and Sicily under the titles of king of the Franks and the Lombards and Roman emperor. He held this vast realm in a grip of iron and cowed its foes on every frontier. He also initiated and encouraged a revival of learning which is sometimes called the Carolingian Renaissance. While this was a brief flash of light in a dark age, it left sparks which made the succeeding period less gloomy and supplied the beginnings of a permanent revival in the twelfth century.

In order to understand the magnitude of Charlemagne's achievement it is necessary to know something of the world into which he

was born. In the fifth and sixth centuries after Christ, Germanic invaders overran the western provinces of the Roman Empire. In the year 700 most of England was ruled by a number of Anglo-Saxon kings, Spain by Visigothic monarchs, and northern and central Italy by the kings of the Lombards. The lands covered today by France and Belgium and the part of Germany known in the Middle Ages as Franconia formed the Frankish state ruled by the kings of the Merovingian line. In 711 Moslems from North Africa overwhelmed the Visigothic kingdom and occupied Spain. Along the eastern frontier of the Frankish state were such Germanic peoples as the Saxons and Bavarians. The plains of the Danube Valley were occupied by a Turkish people called Avars. Southern Italy, Sicily, and a few isolated districts such as Rome and Ravenna recognized the sovereignty of the Byzantine emperor in Constantinople, the successor to the Roman emperors.

Roman civilization had gradually disappeared under the rule of the Germanic kings. Except for Ireland where a few monks still cherished the ancient learning and Northumbria where both Irish and Roman missionaries had fostered a brief revival, Western Europe knew little of bare literacy and practically nothing of real learning. In the Frankish state even the bishops were barely literate.

The economic system of the Roman Empire had also decayed. The Germanic kings had no interest in keeping up roads and bridges and less in policing the trade routes. Overland trade had largely disappeared. The Mediterranean which had formed the heart of the Roman system of communications was harassed by Moslem fleets. As trade declined, the circulation of money grew less and less. By 700 Western Europe was essentially a region of localized agricultural economy. The farmer raised his own raw material and made the crude goods his family needed. The nobles lived on the rents collected from men who farmed their land.

In 700 the Merovingian state was weak and disorganized. The kings were mere figureheads, and the land was ruled by cliques of nobles who fought each other fiercely for power. Its armies were half-armed mobs of little effectiveness in war. While the realm was officially Christian and kings and nobles made generous gifts to churches and monasteries, the clergy were hard to distinguish in life and thought from the secular lords. Christian ethics had as yet had little effect on the ways of the Germans.

Charlemagne's grandfather, Charles Martel, was the head of a victorious noble group. As mayor of the palace, or as he usually called himself *dux* or leader of the Franks, he organized an effective military force by seizing church lands and using them to support soldiers who would serve him as heavily armed cavalry. He repulsed a Moslem invasion and conquered part of Saxony. His successor, Pepin, reorganized the Frankish church with the aid of the great Anglo-Saxon missionary, St. Boniface of Crediton. Pepin removed the last Merovingian king and was himself crowned king, first by St. Boniface and later by Pope Stephen. He drove the Lombards from the vicinity of Rome and gave the government of that region to the pope. This was the origin of the later states of the Church.

Einhard's biography will tell you what Charlemagne accomplished, but it is important to remember the difficulties he faced which Einhard does not mention because he took them for granted. Charlemagne had no revenue in money. He and his court lived on the produce of the royal estates. He supported his officials and his cavalry by giving them land and the labor to farm it. The rest of his army was a general levy of infantry from his subjects. How he succeeded in mustering large armies at distant frontiers and supplying them during long and strenuous campaigns is almost incomprehensible. Just as difficult to understand is how he procured the obedience of his officials scattered over his vast realm. The only possible answer seems to be that he was a man of amazing ability and force of character. We do not need Einhard to show us that Charlemagne was a great man—the chronicles of his reign and the official documents which are still preserved show that. But Einhard gives us a picture of the man and his way of life.

Einhard was born in the ancient Frankish homeland in the valley of the River Main about 775. He was brought up in the monastery of Fulda, which was the chief center of learning in the Frankish lands. In 791 or 792 his abbot persuaded Charlemagne to take him into his court. Early in his reign Charlemagne had gathered men of learning about him and established a palace school headed by a Northumbrian scholar named Alcuin. Soon after Einhard's arrival Alcuin retired to a monastery near Tours. When in 799 Charlemagne asked Alcuin a question about the classics, he told him to consult Einhard. Although Einhard clearly was on intimate terms with Charlemagne and carried out a number of errands for him on affairs of state, he never achieved high office during his reign. But after Charlemagne's death in 814 his son and successor Louis the Pious made Einhard his private secretary and loaded him with honors and benefices. He retired from court in 828, when the quarrels between Louis and his sons grew acute, and lived in a quiet retreat until 840.

Einhard wrote a number of works, but his *Vita Caroli Magni* or *Life of Charlemagne* is by far the most interesting. It was written between 817 and 836, probably between 817 and 830. Einhard made extensive use of the chronicles known as the *annales royales*, which furnished his basic material on Charlemagne's campaigns and political activities. He also consulted works by some of his colleagues in the palace school and documents in the royal archives to which he had access as secretary of Louis the Pious. While he made a number of mistakes in interpreting this material, on the whole his work appears accurate when compared with other sources. Finally, he drew on his own memory of Charlemagne, his character, and his way of life. To the historian this is his great contribution.

When Einhard undertook the task of writing a biography of his patron, he was faced with a serious problem. How did one write a biography? The only models being produced by his contemporaries were lives of saints, and they would hardly serve his purpose. Hence he turned to one of the few classical works available, *De Vita Caesarum,* the *Lives of the Caesars* by the Roman historian Suetonius. He used particularly the biography of Augustus. From this work he took the general form and organization of his work. He also borrowed many descriptive phrases. Some scholars have charged that he used expressions of Suetonius even when they did not really apply to Charlemagne and so distorted his result. The best recent opinion, however, holds that he used Suetonius wisely as a guide and copied only phrases that were appropriate.

Einhard was obviously writing to honor Charlemagne. He clearly passes over delicately various details he considered embarrassing, such as the morals of the king's daughters. Nevertheless, his account has the ring of truth. The Charlemagne he describes could have done what we know he actually did. The biography was immensely popular. Some eighty manuscripts still survive and a number of these were produced in the ninth and tenth centuries. This fame was well deserved. Ein-

hard wrote the first medieval biography of a
lay figure, and his subject was the greatest
man of the age whose memory was revered in
both history and legend throughout the Middle Ages.

CONTENTS

EINHARD'S PREFACE

Since I have taken upon myself to narrate the public and private life, and no small part of the deeds, of my lord and foster-father, the most excellent and most justly renowned King Charles, I have condensed the matter into as brief a form as possible. I have been careful not to omit any facts that could come to my knowledge, but at the same time not to offend by a prolix style those minds that despise everything modern, if one can possibly avoid offending by a new work men who seem to despise also the masterpieces of antiquity, the works of most learned and luminous writers. Very many of them, I have no doubt, are men devoted to a life of literary leisure, who feel that the affairs of the present generation ought not to be passed by, and who do not consider everything done today as unworthy of mention and deserving to be given over to

silence and oblivion, but are nevertheless seduced by lust of immortality to celebrate the
glorious deeds of other times by some sort of
composition rather than to deprive posterity of
the mention of their own names by not writing
at all.

Be this as it may, I see no reason why I
should refrain from entering upon a task of
this kind, since no man can write with more
accuracy than I of events that took place
about me, and of facts concerning which I had
personal knowledge, ocular demonstration, as
the saying goes, and I have no means of ascer-
taining whether or not any one else has the
subject in hand.

In any event, I would rather commit my
story to writing, and hand it down to posterity
in partnership with others, so to speak, than to
suffer the most glorious life of this most excellent king, the greatest of all the princes of his
day, and his illustrious deeds, hard for men
of later times to imitate, to be wrapped in the
darkness of oblivion.

But there are still other reasons, neither
unwarrantable nor insufficient, in my opinion,
that urge me to write on this subject, namely,
the care that King Charles bestowed upon me
in my childhood, and my constant friendship
with himself and his children after I took up

my abode at court. In this way he strongly en-
deared me to himself, and made me greatly his
debtor as well in death as in life, so that were
I, unmindful of the benefits conferred upon
me, to keep silence concerning the most glorious and illustrious deeds of a man who claims
so much at my hands, and suffer his life to lack
due eulogy and written memorial, as if he had
never lived, I should deservedly appear un-
grateful, and be so considered, albeit my
powers are feeble, scanty, next to nothing indeed, and not at all adapted to write and set
forth a life that would tax the eloquence of a
Tully.

I submit the book. It contains the history of
a very great and distinguished man; but there
is nothing in it to wonder at besides his deeds,
except the fact that I, who am a barbarian,
and very little versed in the Roman language,
seem to suppose myself capable of writing
gracefully and respectably in Latin, and to
carry my presumption so far as to disdain the
sentiment that Cicero is said in the first book
of the "Tusculan Disputations" to have expressed when speaking of the Latin authors.
His words are: "It is an outrageous abuse both
of time and literature for a man to commit
his thoughts to writing without having the
ability either to arrange them or elucidate

them, or attract readers by some charm of
style." This dictum of the famous orator might
have deterred me from writing if I had not
made up my mind that it was better to risk the
opinions of the world, and put my little talents
for composition to the test, than to slight the
memory of so great a man for the sake of spar-
ing myself.

EUROPE ACCORDING TO EINHARD

THE LIFE
OF THE EMPEROR CHARLES

1. The Merovingian family, from which the
Franks used to choose their kings, is commonly
said to have lasted until the time of Childeric,[1]
who was deposed, shaved, and thrust into the
cloister by command of the Roman Pontiff
Stephen.[2] But although, to all outward appearance, it ended with him, it had long since been
devoid of vital strength, and conspicuous only
from bearing the empty epithet Royal; the
real power and authority in the kingdom lay
in the hands of the chief officer of the court,
the so-called Mayor of the Palace, and he was
at the head of affairs. There was nothing left
the King to do but to be content with his name
of King, his flowing hair, and long beard,[3] to
sit on his throne and play the ruler, to give ear
to the ambassadors that came from all quar-
ters, and to dismiss them, as if on his own re-
sponsibility, in words that were, in fact, sug-

gested to him, or even imposed upon him. He had nothing that he could call his own beyond this vain title of King and the precarious support allowed by the Mayor of the Palace in his discretion, except a single country seat, that brought him but a very small income. There was a dwelling house upon this, and a small number of servants attached to it, sufficient to perform the necessary offices. When he had to go abroad, he used to ride in a cart, drawn by a yoke of oxen,[4] driven, peasant-fashion, by a ploughman; he rode in this way to the palace and to the general assembly of the people, that met once a year for the welfare of the kingdom, and he returned him in like manner. The Mayor of the Palace took charge of the government and of everything that had to be planned or executed at home or abroad.

II. At the time of Childeric's deposition, Pepin, the father of King Charles, held this office of Mayor of the Palace, one might almost say, by hereditary right; for Pepin's father, *715-41* Charles, had received it at the hands of his father, Pepin, and filled it with distinction. It was this Charles that crushed the tyrants who claimed to rule the whole Frank land as their own, and that utterly routed the Saracens, when they attempted the conquest of Gaul, in two great battles—one in Aquitania, near the

town of Poitiers, and the other on the River
Berre,⁵ near Narbonne—and compelled them
to return to Spain. This honor was usually
conferred by the people only upon men emi-
nent from their illustrious birth and ample
wealth. For some years, ostensibly under King
Childeric, Pepin, the father of King Charles,
shared the duties inherited from his father and
grandfather most amicably with his brother,
Carloman. The latter, then, for reasons unknown, renounced the heavy cares of an
earthly crown and retired to Rome. Here he   *747*
exchanged his worldly garb for a cowl, and
built a monastery on Mt. Oreste, near the
Church of St. Sylvester, where he enjoyed for
several years the seclusion that he desired, in
company with certain others who had the
same object in view. But so many distinguished Franks made the pilgrimage to Rome
to fulfill their vows, and insisted upon paying
their respects to him, as their former lord, on
the way, that the repose which he so much
loved was broken by these frequent visits, and
he was driven to change his abode. Accordingly, when he found that his plans were frus-
trated by his many visitors, he abandoned
the mountain, and withdrew to the Monastery
of St. Benedict, on Monte Cassino, in the   *754*
province of Samnium, and passed the rest

of his days there in the exercises of religion.

III. Pepin, however, was raised, by decree of the Roman Pontiff, from the rank of Mayor of the Palace to that of King, and ruled alone over the Franks for fifteen years or more.[6] He died of dropsy, in Paris, at the close of the Aquitanian war,[7] which he had waged with William, Duke of Aquitania, for nine successive years, and left two sons, Charles and Carloman, upon whom, by the grace of God, the succession devolved.

752–68

Sept. 24, 768

760–68

The Franks, in a general assembly of the people, made them both kings, on condition that they should divide the whole kingdom equally between them, Charles to take and rule the part that had belonged to their father, Pepin, and Carloman the part which their uncle, Carloman, had governed.[8] The conditions were accepted, and each entered into possession of the share of the kingdom that fell to him by this arrangement; but peace was only maintained between them with the greatest difficulty, because many of Carloman's party kept trying to disturb their good understanding, and there were some even who plotted to involve them in a war with each other. The event, however, showed the danger to have been rather imaginary than real, for at Carloman's death his widow[9] fled to Italy with

Oct. 9, 768

her sons[10] and her principal adherents, and without reason, despite her husband's brother, put herself and her children under the protection of Desiderius, King of the Lombards. Carloman had succumbed to disease after ruling two years[11] in common with his brother, and at his death Charles was unanimously elected King of the Franks.

IV. It would be folly, I think, to write a word concerning Charles' birth[12] and infancy, or even his boyhood, for nothing has ever been written on the subject, and there is no one alive now who can give information of it. Accordingly, I have determined to pass that by as unknown, and to proceed at once to treat of his character, his deeds, and such other facts of his life as are worth telling and setting forth, and shall first give an account of his deeds at home and abroad, then of his character and pursuits, and lastly of his administration and death, omitting nothing worth knowing or necessary to know.

V. His first undertaking in a military way was the Aquitanian war,[13] begun by his father, but not brought to a close; and because he thought that it could be readily carried through, he took it up while his brother was yet alive, calling upon him to render aid. The campaign once opened, he conducted it with

the greatest vigor, notwithstanding his brother
withheld the assistance that he had promised,
and did not desist or shrink from his self-im-
posed task until, by his patience and firmness,
he had completely gained his ends. He compelled Hunold, who had attempted to seize
Aquitania after Waifar's death, and renew
the war then almost concluded, to abandon
Aquitania and flee to Gascony. Even here he
gave him no rest, but crossed the River
Garonne, built the castle of Fronsac, and sent
ambassadors to Lupus, Duke of Gascony, to
demand the surrender of the fugitive, threat-
ening to take him by force unless he were
promptly given up to him. Thereupon Lupus
chose the wiser course, and not only gave
Hunold up, but submitted himself, with the
province which he ruled, to the King.

vi. After bringing this war to an end and
settling matters in Aquitania (his associate in
authority had meantime departed this life),
he was induced, by the prayers and entreaties
773   of Hadrian,[14] Bishop of the city of Rome, to
wage war on the Lombards. His father before
him had undertaken this task at the request
of Pope Stephen,[15] but under great difficulties,
for certain leading Franks, of whom he usually
took counsel, had so vehemently opposed his
design as to declare openly that they would

leave the King and go home. Nevertheless, the war against the Lombard King Astolf had been taken up and very quickly concluded. *754*

Now, although Charles seems to have had similar, or rather just the same grounds for declaring war that his father had, the war itself differed from the preceding one alike in its difficulties and its issue. Pepin, to be sure, after besieging King Astolf a few days in Pavia, had compelled him to give hostages, to restore to the Romans the cities and castles that he had taken, and to make oath that he would not attempt to seize them again: but Charles did not cease, after declaring war, until he had exhausted King Desiderius by a long siege, and forced him to surrender at discretion; driven his son Adalgis, the last hope of the Lombards, not only from his kingdom, but from all Italy; restored to the Romans all that they had lost; subdued Hruodgaus, Duke of Friuli, who was plotting revolution; reduced all Italy to his power, and set his son Pepin as king over it. *781*

773

774

776

At this point I should describe Charles' difficult passage over the Alps into Italy, and the hardships that the Franks endured in climbing the trackless mountain ridges, the heaven-aspiring cliffs and ragged peaks, if it were not my purpose in this work to record the manner of his life rather than the incidents of the wars that he waged. Suffice it to say that this war ended with the subjection of Italy, the banishment of King Desiderius for life, the expulsion of his son Adalgis from Italy, and the restoration of the conquests of the Lombard kings to Hadrian, the head of the Roman Church.

VII. At the conclusion of this struggle, the Saxon war, that seems to have been only laid aside for the time, was taken up again. No war ever undertaken by the Frank nation was carried on with such persistence and bitterness, or cost so much labor, because the Saxons, like almost all the tribes of Germany, were a fierce people, given to the worship of devils, and hostile to our religion, and did not consider it dishonorable to transgress and violate all law, human and divine. Then there were peculiar circumstances that tended to cause a breach of peace every day. Except in a few places, where large forests or mountain ridges intervened and made the bounds certain, the line between ourselves and the Saxons passed almost in its whole extent through an open country, so that there was no end to the murders, thefts, and arsons on both sides. In this way the Franks 772 became so embittered that they at last resolved to make reprisals no longer, but to come to open war with the Saxons. Accordingly war was begun against them, and was waged for thirty-three successive years with great fury; more, however, to the disadvantage of the Saxons than of the Franks. It could doubtless have been brought to an end sooner, had it not been for the faithlessness of the Saxons. It is hard to say how often they were conquered, and, humbly submitting to the King, promised to do what was enjoined upon them, gave without hesitation the required hostages, and received the officers sent them from the King. They were sometimes so much weakened and reduced that they promised to renounce the worship of devils, and to adopt Christianity, but they were no less ready to violate these terms than prompt to accept them, so that it is impossible to tell which came easier to them to do; scarcely a year passed from the beginning of the war without such changes on their part. But the King did not suffer his high purpose and steadfastness— firm alike in good and evil fortune—to be wearied by any fickleness on their part, or to be turned from the task that he had undertaken; on the contrary, he never allowed their faithless behavior to go unpunished, but either took the field against them in person, or sent his counts with an army to wreak vengeance[16] and exact righteous satisfaction. At last, after

conquering and subduing all who had offered
resistance, he took ten thousand of those that
804   lived on the banks of the Elbe, and settled
them, with their wives and children, in many
different bodies here and there in Gaul and
Germany. The war that had lasted so many
years was at length ended by their acceding
to the terms offered by the King; which were
renunciation of their national religious customs and the worship of devils, acceptance of
the sacraments of the Christian faith and religion, and union with the Franks to form one
people.

VIII. Charles himself fought but two pitched
battles in this war, although it was long pro-
783   tracted—one on Mount Osning,[17] at the place
called Detmold, and again on the bank of the
river Hase,[18] both in the space of little more
than a month. The enemy were so routed and
overthrown in these two battles that they
never afterwards ventured to take the offen-
sive or to resist the attacks of the King, unless
they were protected by a strong position. A
great many of the Frank as well as of the
Saxon nobility, men occupying the highest
posts of honor, perished in this war, which only
804   came to an end after the lapse of thirty-two
years. So many and grievous were the wars
that were declared against the Franks in the

meantime, and skillfully conducted by the King, that one may reasonably question whether his fortitude or his good fortune is to be more admired. The Saxon war began two years before the Italian war;[19] but although it went on without interruption, business elsewhere was not neglected, nor was there any shrinking from other equally arduous contests. The King, who excelled all the princes of his time in wisdom and greatness of soul, did not suffer difficulty to deter him or danger to daunt him from anything that had to be taken up or carried through, for he had trained himself to bear and endure whatever came, without yielding in adversity, or trusting to the deceitful favors of fortune in prosperity.

IX. In the midst of this vigorous and almost uninterrupted struggle with the Saxons, he covered the frontier by garrisons at the proper points, and marched over the Pyrenees into Spain at the head of all the forces that he could muster. All the towns and castles that he attacked surrendered, and up to the time of his homeward march he sustained no loss whatever; but on his return through the Pyrenees he had cause to rue the treachery of the Gascons. That region is well adapted for ambuscades by reason of the thick forests that cover it; and as the army was advancing in the long

778

line of march necessitated by the narrowness of the road, the Gascons, who lay in ambush *778* on the top of a very high mountain, attacked the rear of the baggage train and the rear guard in charge of it, and hurled them down to the very bottom of the valley.[20] In the struggle that ensued, they cut them off to a man; they then plundered the baggage, and dispersed with all speed in every direction under cover of approaching night. The lightness of their armor and the nature of the battle ground stood the Gascons in good stead on this occasion, whereas the Franks fought at a disadvantage in every respect, because of the weight of their armor and the unevenness of the ground. Eggihard, the King's steward; Anselm, Count Palatine; and Roland,[21] Governor of the March of Brittany, with very many others, fell in this engagement. This ill turn could not be avenged for the nonce, because the enemy scattered so widely after carrying out their plan that not the least clue could be had to their whereabouts.

x. Charles also subdued the Bretons, who *786* live on the sea coast, in the extreme western part of Gaul. When they refused to obey him, he sent an army against them, and compelled them to give hostages, and to promise to do his bidding. He afterwards entered Italy in person

with his army, and passed through Rome to 787
Capua, a city in Campania, where he pitched
his camp and threatened the Beneventans with
hostilities unless they should submit themselves to him. Their duke, Aragis, escaped the
danger by sending his two sons, Rumold and
Grimold, with a great sum of money to meet
the King, begging him to accept them as hostages, and promising for himself and his people
compliance with all the King's commands, on
the single condition that his personal attend-
ance should not be required. The King took
the welfare of the people into account rather
than the stubborn disposition of the Duke, accepted the proffered hostages, and released
him from the obligation to appear before him
in consideration of his handsome gift. He re-
tained the younger son only as hostage, and
sent the elder back to his father, and returned
to Rome, leaving commissioners with Aragis to
exact the oath of allegiance, and administer it
to the Beneventans. He stayed in Rome several days in order to pay his devotions at the
holy places, and then came back to Gaul. 787

XI. At this time, on a sudden, the Bavarian
war broke out, but came to a speedy end. It
was due to the arrogance and folly of Duke
Tassilo. His wife,[22] a daughter of King Desiderius, was desirous of avenging her father's

banishment through the agency of her husband, and accordingly induced him to make a treaty with the Huns, the neighbors of the Bavarians on the east, and not only to leave the King's commands unfulfilled, but to challenge him to war. Charles' high spirit could not brook Tassilo's insubordination, for it seemed to him to pass all bounds; accordingly he straightway summoned his troops from all sides for a campaign against Bavaria, and appeared in person with a great army on the river Lech, which forms the boundary between the Bavarians and the Alemanni. After pitching his camp upon its banks, he determined to put the Duke's disposition to the test by an embassy before entering the province. Tassilo did not think that it was for his own or his people's good to persist, so he surrendered himself to the King, gave the hostages demanded, among them his own son Theodo, and promised by oath not to give ear to any one who should attempt to turn him from his allegiance; so this war, which bade fair to be very grievous, came very quickly to an end. Tassilo, however, was afterward summoned to the King's presence, and not suffered to depart, and the government of the province that he had had in charge was no longer intrusted to a duke, but to counts.

xii. After these uprisings had been thus quelled, war was declared against the Slavs *789* who are commonly known among us as Wilzi, but properly, that is to say in their own tongue, are called Welatabians. The Saxons served in this campaign as auxiliaries among the tribes that followed the King's standard at his summons, but their obedience lacked sincerity and devotion. War was declared because the Slavs kept harassing the Abodriti, old allies of the Franks, by continual raids, in spite of all commands to the contrary. A gulf[23] of unknown length, but nowhere more than a hundred miles wide, and in many parts narrower, stretches off towards the east from the Western Ocean. Many tribes have settlements on its shores; the Danes and Swedes, whom we call Northmen, on the northern shore and all the adjacent islands; but the southern shore is inhabited by the Slavs and Aïsti,[24] and various other tribes. The Welatabians, against whom the King now made war, were the chief of these; but in a single campaign, which he conducted in person, he so crushed and sub- *789* dued them that they did not think it advisable thereafter to refuse obedience to his commands.

xiii. The war against the Avars, or Huns,[25] followed, and, except the Saxon war, was the *791* greatest that he waged; he took it up with more spirit than any of his other wars, and *791* made far greater preparations for it. He conducted one campaign in person in Pannonia, of which the Huns then had possession. He intrusted all subsequent operations to his son, Pepin, and the governors of the provinces, to counts even, and lieutenants. Although they most vigorously prosecuted the war, it only came to a conclusion after a seven years' struggle. The utter depopulation of Pannonia, and the site of the Khan's palace, now a desert, where not a trace of human habitation is visible, bear witness how many battles were fought in those years, and how much blood was shed. The entire body of the Hun nobility perished in this contest, and all its glory with it. All the money and treasure that had been years amassing was seized, and no war in which the Franks have ever engaged within the memory of man brought them such riches and such booty. Up to that time the Huns had passed[26] for a poor people, but so much gold and silver was found in the Khan's palace, and so much valuable spoil taken in battle, that one may well think that the Franks took justly from the Huns what the Huns had formerly taken unjustly from other nations. Only two of the chief men of the Franks fell in this war

—Eric, Duke of Friuli, who was killed in   *799*
Tarsatch,[27] a town on the coast of Liburnia, by
the treachery of the inhabitants; and Gerold,[28]
Governor of Bavaria, who met his death in
Pannonia, slain, with two men that were ac-   *799*
companying him, by an unknown hand while
he was marshaling his forces for battle against
the Huns, and riding up and down the line en-
couraging his men. This war was otherwise
almost a bloodless one so far as the Franks
were concerned, and ended most satisfactorily,
although by reason of its magnitude it was
long protracted.

xiv. The Saxon war next came to an end as
successful as the struggle had been long. The   *804*
Bohemian and Linonian wars[29] that next broke
out could not last long; both were quickly car-   *805–8*
ried through under the leadership of the
younger Charles. The last of these wars was
the one declared against the Northmen called
Danes. They began their career as pirates, but
afterward took to laying waste the coasts of
Gaul and Germany with their large fleet. Their
King Godfred was so puffed with vain aspira-
tions that he counted on gaining empire over
all Germany, and looked upon Saxony and
Frisia as his provinces. He had already subdued his neighbors the Abodriti, and made
them tributary, and boasted that he would

shortly appear with a great army before Aix-
la-Chapelle, where the King held his court.
Some faith was put in his words, empty as they
sound, and it is supposed that he would have
attempted something of the sort if he had not
been prevented by a premature death. He was
810 murdered by one of his own bodyguard, and
so ended at once his life and the war that he
had begun.

xv. Such are the wars, most skilfully
planned and successfully fought, which this
most powerful king waged during the forty-
seven years of his reign.[30] He so largely increased the Frank kingdom, which was already
great and strong when he received it at his
father's hands, that more than double its
former territory was added to it. The authority of the Franks was formerly confined to that
part of Gaul included between the Rhine and
the Loire, the Ocean and the Balearic Sea; to
that part of Germany which is inhabited by
the so-called Eastern Franks, and is bounded
by Saxony and the Danube, the Rhine and the
Saale—this stream separates the Thuringians
from the Sorabians; and to the country of the
Alemanni and Bavarians. By the wars above
mentioned he first made tributary Aquitania,
Gascony, and the whole of the region of the
Pyrenees as far as the River Ebro, which rises

in the land of the Navarrese, flows through the most fertile districts of Spain, and empties into the Balearic Sea, beneath the walls of the city of Tortosa. He next reduced and made tributary all Italy from Aosta to Lower Calabria, where the boundary line runs between the Beneventans and the Greeks, a territory more than a thousand miles[31] long; then Saxony, which constitutes no small part of Germany, and is reckoned to be twice as wide as the country inhabited by the Franks, while about equal to it in length; in addition, both Pannonias, Dacia beyond the Danube, and Istria, Liburnia, and Dalmatia, except the cities on the coast, which he left to the Greek Emperor for friendship's sake, and because of the treaty that he had made with him. In fine, he vanquished and made tributary all the wild and barbarous tribes dwelling in Germany between the Rhine and the Vistula, the Ocean and the Danube, all of which speak very much the same language, but differ widely from one another in customs and dress. The chief among them are the Welatabians, the Sorabians, the Abodriti, and the Bohemians, and he had to make war upon these; but the rest, by far the larger number, submitted to him of their own accord.

xvi. He added to the glory of his reign by

gaining the good will of several kings and nations; so close, indeed, was the alliance that he
contracted with Alfonso,[32] King of Galicia and
Asturias, that the latter, when sending letters
or ambassadors to Charles, invariably styled
himself his man. His munificence won the
kings of the Scots also to pay such deference
to his wishes that they never gave him any
other title than lord, or themselves than subjects and slaves: there are letters from them
extant[33] in which these feelings in his regard
are expressed. His relations with Aaron,[34] King
of the Persians, who ruled over almost the
whole of the East, India excepted, were so
friendly that this prince preferred his favor to
that of all the kings and potentates of the
earth, and considered that to him alone marks
of honor and munificence were due. Accordingly, when the ambassadors sent by Charles
to visit the most holy sepulchre and place of
resurrection of our Lord and Savior presented
themselves before him with gifts, and made
known their master's wishes, he not only
granted what was asked, but gave possession
of that holy and blessed spot. When they returned, he dispatched his ambassadors with
them, and sent magnificent gifts, besides stuffs,
perfumes, and other rich products of the Eastern lands. A few years before this, Charles had

asked him for an elephant, and he sent the only one that he had. The Emperors of Constantinople, Nicephorus,[35] Michael,[36] and Leo,[37] made advances to Charles, and sought friendship and alliance with him by several embassies; and even when the Greeks suspected him of designing to wrest the empire from them, because of his assumption of the title Emperor, they made a close alliance with him, that he might have no cause of offense. In fact, the power of the Franks was always viewed by the Greeks and Romans with a jealous eye, whence the Greek proverb "Have the Frank for your friend, but not for your neighbor."

XVII. This King, who showed himself so great in extending his empire and subduing foreign nations, and was constantly occupied with plans to that end, undertook also very many works calculated to adorn and benefit his kingdom, and brought several of them to completion. Among these, the most deserving of mention are the basilica of the Holy Mother of God at Aix-la-Chapelle, built in the most admirable manner, and a bridge over the Rhine at Mayence, half a mile long, the breadth of the river at this point. This bridge was destroyed by fire the year before Charles died, but, owing to his death so soon after, could

May, 813

not be repaired, although he had intended to rebuild it in stone. He began two palaces[38] of beautiful workmanship—one near his manor called Ingelheim, not far from Mayence; the other at Nimeguen, on the Waal, the stream that washes the south side of the island of the Batavians. But, above all, sacred edifices were the object of his care throughout his whole kingdom; and whenever he found them falling to ruin from age, he commanded the priests and fathers who had charge of them to repair them, and made sure by commissioners that his instructions were obeyed. He also fitted out a fleet for the war with the Northmen; the vessels required for this purpose were built on the rivers that flow from Gaul and Germany into the Northern Ocean. Moreover, since the Northmen continually overran and laid waste the Gallic and German coasts, he caused watch and ward to be kept in all the harbors, and at the mouths of rivers large enough to admit the entrance of vessels, to prevent the enemy from disembarking; and in the South, in Narbonensis and Septimania, and along the whole coast of Italy as far as Rome, he took the same precautions against the Moors, who had recently begun their piratical practices. Hence, Italy suffered no great harm in his time at the hands of the Moors, nor Gaul and Germany from the

Northmen, save that the Moors got possession of the Etruscan town of Civita Vecchia by treachery, and sacked it, and the Northmen harried some of the islands in Frisia off the German coast.

XVIII. Thus did Charles defend and increase as well as beautify his kingdom, as is well known; and here let me express my admiration of his great qualities and his extraordinary constancy alike in good and evil fortune. I will now forthwith proceed to give the details of his private and family life.

After his father's death, while sharing the kingdom with his brother, he bore his unfriendliness and jealousy most patiently, and, to the *768–71* wonder of all, could not be provoked to be angry with him. Later he married a daughter[39] *770* of Desiderius, King of the Lombards, at the instance of his mother; but he repudiated her at the end of a year for some reason unknown, and married Hildegard, a woman of high birth, of Suabian origin. He had three sons by her— *771* Charles, Pepin,[40] and Louis[41]—and as many daughters[42]—Hruodrud,[43] Bertha,[44] and Gisela. He had three other daughters besides these— Theoderada,[45] Hiltrud,[46] and Ruodhaid—two by his third wife, Fastrada, a woman of East Frankish[47] (that is to say, of German) origin, and the third by a concubine, whose name for

the moment escapes me.[48] At the death of
794 Fastrada, he married Liutgard, an Alemannic
woman, who bore him no children. After her
June 4, death he had three concubines[49]—Gersuinda,
800 a Saxon, by whom he had Adaltrud; Regina,
who was the mother of Drogo and Hugh;[50] and
Ethelind, by whom he had Theodoric.[51]
Charles' mother, Berthrada, passed her old
age with him in great honor; he entertained
the greatest veneration for her; and there was
never any disagreement between them except
when he divorced the daughter of King Desiderius, whom he had married to please her. She
783 died soon after Hildegard, after living to see
three grandsons and as many granddaughters
in her son's house, and he buried her with great
pomp in the Basilica of St. Denis, where his
father lay. He had an only sister,[52] Gisela, who
had consecrated herself to a religious life from
girlhood, and he cherished as much affection
810 for her as for his mother. She also died a few
years before him in the nunnery where she
had passed her life.[53]

xix. The plan that he adopted for his children's education was, first of all, to have both
boys and girls instructed in the liberal arts, to
which he also turned his own attention. As
soon as their years admitted, in accordance
with the custom of the Franks, the boys had to

learn horsemanship, and to practice war and the chase, and the girls to familiarize themselves with cloth-making, and to handle distaff and spindle, that they might not grow indolent through idleness, and he fostered in them every virtuous sentiment. He only lost three of all his children before his death, two sons and one daughter, Charles, who was the eldest, Pepin, whom he had made King of Italy, and Hruodrud, his oldest daughter, whom he had betrothed to Constantine,[54] Emperor of the Greeks. Pepin left one son, named Bernard,[55] and five daughters, Adelaide, Atula, Guntrada, Berthaid, and Theoderada. The King gave a striking proof of his fatherly affection at the *810* time of Pepin's death: he appointed the grandson to succeed Pepin, and had the granddaughters brought up with his own daughters. When *813* his sons and his daughter died, he was not so calm as might have been expected from his remarkably strong mind, for his affections were no less strong, and moved him to tears. Again, when he was told of the death of Hadrian, the *796* Roman Pontiff, whom he had loved most of all his friends, he wept as much as if he had lost a brother, or a very dear son. He was by nature most ready to contract friendships, and not only made friends easily, but clung to them persistently, and cherished most fondly those

with whom he had formed such ties. He was so
careful of the training of his sons and daughters that he never took his meals without them
when he was at home, and never made a journey without them; his sons would ride at his
side, and his daughters follow him, while a
number of his bodyguard, detailed for their
protection, brought up the rear. Strange to
say, although they were very handsome wom-
en, and he loved them very dearly, he was
never willing to marry[56] any of them to a man
of their own nation or to a foreigner, but kept
them all at home until his death, saying that
he could not dispense with their society.
Hence, though otherwise happy, he experi-
enced the malignity of fortune as far as they
were concerned; yet he concealed his knowledge of the rumors current in regard to them,
and of the suspicions entertained of their
honor.[57]

xx. By one of his concubines[58] he had a
son, handsome in face, but hunchbacked,
named Pepin, whom I omitted to mention in
the list of his children. When Charles was at
war with the Huns, and was wintering in
_792_ Bavaria, this Pepin shammed sickness, and
plotted against his father in company with
some of the leading Franks, who seduced him
with vain promises of the royal authority.

When his deceit was discovered, and the con-
spirators were punished, his head was shaved,
and he was suffered, in accordance with his
wishes, to devote himself to a religious life in
the monastery of Prüm. A formidable con-
spiracy against Charles had previously been *785–86*
set on foot in Germany, but all the traitors
were banished, some of them without mutila-
tion, others after their eyes had been put out.
Three of them only lost their lives; they drew
their swords and resisted arrest, and, after
killing several men, were cut down, because
they could not be otherwise overpowered. It is
supposed that the cruelty of Queen Fastrada
was the primary cause of these plots, and they
were both due to Charles' apparent acquies-
cence in his wife's cruel conduct, and deviation
from the usual kindness and gentleness of his
disposition. All the rest of his life he was re-
garded by everyone with the utmost love and
affection, so much so that not the least accusa-
tion of unjust rigor was ever made against him.

xxi. He liked foreigners, and was at great
pains to take them under his protection. There
were often so many of them, both in the palace
and the kingdom, that they might reasonably
have been considered a nuisance; but he, with
his broad humanity, was very little disturbed
by such annoyances, because he felt himself

compensated for these great inconveniences by
the praises of his generosity and the reward of
high renown.

XXII. Charles was large and strong, and of
lofty stature, though not disproportionately
tall (his height is well known to have been
seven times the length of his foot); the upper
part of his head was round, his eyes very large
and animated, nose a little long, hair fair, and
face laughing and merry. Thus his appearance
was always stately and dignified, whether he
was standing or sitting; although his neck was
thick and somewhat short, and his belly rather
prominent; but the symmetry of the rest of his
body concealed these defects. His gait was
firm, his whole carriage manly, and his voice
clear, but not so strong as his size led one to
expect. His health was excellent, except during the four years preceding his death, when
he was subject to frequent fevers; at the last
he even limped a little with one foot. Even in
those years he consulted rather his own in-
clinations than the advice of physicians, who
were almost hateful to him, because they
wanted him to give up roasts, to which he was
accustomed, and to eat boiled meat instead. In
accordance with the national custom, he took
frequent exercise on horseback and in the
chase, accomplishments in which scarcely any

people in the world can equal the Franks. He enjoyed the exhalations from natural warm springs, and often practiced swimming, in which he was such an adept that none could surpass him; and hence it was that he built his palace at Aix-la-Chapelle, and lived there constantly during his latter years until his death. He used not only to invite his sons to his bath, but his nobles and friends, and now and then a troop of his retinue or bodyguard, so that a hundred or more persons sometimes bathed with him.

XXIII. He used to wear the national, that is to say, the Frank, dress—next his skin a linen shirt and linen breeches, and above these a tunic fringed with silk; while hose fastened by bands covered his lower limbs, and shoes his feet, and he protected his shoulders and chest in winter by a close-fitting coat of otter or marten skins. Over all he flung a blue cloak, and he always had a sword girt about him, usually one with a gold or silver hilt and belt; he sometimes carried a jeweled sword, but only on great feastdays or at the reception of ambassadors from foreign nations. He despised foreign costumes, however handsome, and never allowed himself to be robed in them, except twice in Rome, when he donned the Roman tunic, chlamys, and shoes; the first time at the request of Pope Hadrian,[59] the second to gratify Leo,[60] Hadrian's successor. On great feastdays he made use of embroidered clothes and shoes bedecked with precious stones, his cloak was fastened by a golden buckle, and he appeared crowned with a diadem of gold and gems, but on other days his dress varied little from the common dress of the people.

XXIV. Charles was temperate in eating, and particularly so in drinking, for he abominated drunkenness in anybody, much more in himself and those of his household; but he could not easily abstain from food, and often complained that fasts injured his health. He very rarely gave entertainments, only on great feastdays, and then to large numbers of people. His meals ordinarily consisted of four courses, not counting the roast, which his huntsmen used to bring in on the spit; he was more fond of this than of any other dish. While at table, he listened to reading or music. The subjects of the readings were the stories and deeds of olden time: he was fond, too, of St. Augustine's books, and especially of the one entitled "The City of God." He was so moderate in the use of wine and all sorts of drink that he rarely allowed himself more than three cups in the course of a meal. In summer, after the midday meal, he would eat some fruit, drain a single cup, put off his clothes and shoes, just as he did for the night, and rest for two or three hours. He was in the habit of awaking and rising from bed four or five times during the night. While he was dressing and putting on his shoes, he not only gave audience to his friends, but if the Count of the Palace told him of any suit in which his judgment was necessary, he had the parties brought before him forthwith, took cognizance of the case, and gave his decision, just as if he were sitting on the judgment seat. This was not the only business that he transacted at this time, but he performed any duty of the day whatever, whether he had to attend to the matter himself, or to give commands concerning it to his officers.

xxv. Charles had the gift of ready and fluent speech, and could express whatever he had to say with the utmost clearness. He was not satisfied with command of his native language merely, but gave attention to the study of foreign ones, and in particular was such a master of Latin that he could speak it as well as his native tongue; but he could understand Greek better than he could speak it. He was so eloquent, indeed, that he might have passed for a teacher of eloquence. He most zealously

cultivated the liberal arts, held those who
taught them in great esteem, and conferred
great honors upon them. He took lessons in
grammar of the deacon Peter of Pisa,[61] at that
time an aged man. Another deacon, Albin of
Britain, surnamed Alcuin,[62] a man of Saxon
extraction, who was the greatest scholar of
the day, was his teacher in other branches of
learning. The King spent much time and labor
with him studying rhetoric, dialectics, and especially astronomy; he learned to reckon, and
used to investigate the motions of the heaven-
ly bodies most curiously, with an intelligent
scrutiny. He also tried to write, and used to
keep tablets and blanks in bed under his pil-
low, that at leisure hours he might accustom
his hand to form the letters; however, as he
did not begin his efforts in due season, but late
in life, they met with ill success.

xxvi. He cherished with the greatest fervor
and devotion the principles of the Christian
religion, which had been instilled into him
from infancy. Hence it was that he built the
beautiful basilica at Aix-la-Chapelle, which he
adorned with gold and silver and lamps, and
with rails and doors of solid brass. He had the
columns and marbles for this structure brought
from Rome and Ravenna,[63] for he could not
find such as were suitable elsewhere. He was

a constant worshipper at this church as long
as his health permitted, going morning and
evening, even after nightfall, besides attend-
ing mass; and he took care that all the services
there conducted should be administered with
the utmost possible propriety, very often
warning the sextons not to let any improper
or unclean thing be brought into the building
or remain in it. He provided it with a great
number of sacred vessels of gold and silver
and with such a quantity of clerical robes that
not even the doorkeepers who fill the humblest
office in the church were obliged to wear their
everyday clothes when in the exercise of their
duties. He was at great pains to improve the
church reading and psalmody, for he was well
skilled in both, although he neither read in
public nor sang, except in a low tone and with
others.

XXVII. He was very forward in succoring
the poor, and in that gratuitous generosity
which the Greeks call alms, so much so that he
not only made a point of giving in his own
country and his own kingdom, but when he
discovered that there were Christians living
in poverty in Syria, Egypt, and Africa, at
Jerusalem, Alexandria, and Carthage, he had
compassion on their wants, and used to send
money over the seas to them. The reason that

he zealously strove to make friends with the
kings beyond seas was that he might get help
and relief to the Christians living under their
rule. He cherished the Church of St. Peter the
Apostle at Rome above all other holy and
sacred places, and heaped its treasury with a
vast wealth of gold, silver, and precious stones.
He sent great and countless gifts to the popes,
and throughout his whole reign the wish that
he had nearest at heart was to re-establish the
ancient authority of the city of Rome under
his care and by his influence, and to defend
and protect the Church of St. Peter, and to
beautify and enrich it out of his own store
above all other churches. Although he held it
in such veneration, he only repaired to Rome
to pay his vows and make his supplications
four times[64] during the whole forty-seven
years[65] that he reigned.

XXVIII. When he made his last journey
thither, he had also other ends in view. The
Romans had inflicted many injuries upon the
Pontiff Leo, tearing out his eyes and cutting
out his tongue, so that he had been compelled
to call upon the King for help. Charles accordingly went to Rome, to set in order the affairs
of the Church, which were in great confusion,
and passed the whole winter there. It was then
that he received the titles of Emperor and

Nov. 24, 800

Dec. 25, 800

Augustus, to which he at first had such an aversion that he declared that he would not have set foot in the Church the day that they were conferred, although it was a great feast-day, if he could have foreseen the design of the Pope. He bore very patiently with the jealousy which the Roman emperors showed upon his assuming these titles, for they took this step very ill; and by dint of frequent embassies and letters, in which he addressed them as brothers, he made their haughtiness yield to his magnanimity, a quality in which he was unquestionably much their superior.

xxix. It was after he had received the imperial name that, finding the laws of his people very defective (the Franks have two sets of laws,[66] very different in many particulars), he determined to add what was wanting, to reconcile the discrepancies, and to correct what was vicious and wrongly cited in them. However, he went no further in this matter than to supplement the laws by a few capitularies, and those imperfect ones; but he caused the unwritten laws of all the tribes that came under his rule[67] to be compiled and reduced to writing. He also had the old rude songs that celebrate the deeds and wars of the ancient kings written out for transmission to posterity. He began a grammar of his native language. He

gave the months names in his own tongue, in
place of the Latin and barbarous names by
which they were formerly known among the
Franks. He likewise designated the winds by
twelve appropriate names; there were hardly
more than four distinctive ones in use before.
He called January, Wintarmanoth;[68] Febru-
ary, Hornung;[69] March, Lentzinmanoth;[70]
April, Ostarmanoth;[71] May, Winnemanoth;[72]
June, Brachmanoth;[73] July, Heuvimanoth;[74]
August, Aranmanoth;[75] September, Wituma-
noth;[76] October, Windumemanoth;[77] November, Herbistmanoth;[78] December, Heilagma-
noth.[79] He styled the winds as follows; Sub-
solanus, Ostroniwint; Eurus, Ostsundroni;
Euroauster, Sundostroni; Auster, Sundroni;
Austro-Africus, Sundwestroni; Africus, West-
sundroni; Zephyrus, Westroni; Caurus, West-
nordroni; Circius, Nordwestroni; Septentrio,
Nordroni; Aquilo, Nordostroni; Vulturnus,
Ostnordroni.[80]

xxx. Toward the close of his life, when he
was broken by ill-health and old age, he sum-
813   moned Louis, King of Aquitania, his only surviving son by Hildegard, and gathered together all the chief men of the whole kingdom of
the Franks in a solemn assembly. He appointed Louis, with their unanimous consent,
to rule with himself over the whole kingdom,

and constituted him heir to the imperial name; then, placing the diadem upon his son's head, he bade him be proclaimed Emperor and Augustus. This step was hailed by all present with great favor, for it really seemed as if God had prompted him to it for the kingdom's good; it increased the King's dignity, and struck no little terror into foreign nations. After sending his son back to Aquitania, although weak from age he set out to hunt, as usual, near his palace at Aix-la-Chapelle, and passed the rest of the autumn in the chase, returning thither about the first of November. *Nov. 1, 813* While wintering there, he was seized, in the month of January, with a high fever, and took to his bed. As soon as he was taken sick, he *Jan. 22, 814* prescribed for himself abstinence from food, as he always used to do in case of fever, thinking that the disease could be driven off, or at least mitigated, by fasting. Besides the fever, he suffered from a pain in the side, which the Greeks call pleurisy; but he still persisted in fasting, and in keeping up his strength only by draughts taken at very long intervals. He died January twenty-eighth, the seventh day from *Jan. 28, 814* the time that he took to his bed, at nine o'clock in the morning, after partaking of the holy communion, in the seventy-second year of his age[81] and the forty-seventh of his reign.

XXXI. His body was washed and cared for in
the usual manner, and was then carried to the
church, and interred amid the greatest lamen-
tations of all the people. There was some question at first where to lay him, because in his
lifetime he had given no directions as to his
burial; but at length all agreed that he could
nowhere be more honorably entombed than in
the very basilica that he had built in the town
at his own expense, for love of God and our
Lord Jesus Christ, and in honor of the Holy
and Eternal Virgin, His Mother. He was
buried there the same day that he died, and a
gilded arch was erected above his tomb with
his image and an inscription. The words of the
inscription were as follows: "In this tomb lies
the body of Charles, the Great and Orthodox
Emperor, who gloriously extended the kingdom of the Franks, and reigned prosperously
for forty-seven years.[82] He died at the age of
seventy, in the year of our Lord 814, the 7th
Indiction, on the 28th day of January."

XXXII. Very many omens had portended his
approaching end, a fact that he had recognized
as well as others. Eclipses both of the sun and
moon were very frequent during the last three
years of his life, and a black spot was visible
on the sun for the space of seven days. The
gallery between the basilica and the palace,

which he had built at great pains and labor,
fell in sudden ruin to the ground on the day of
the Ascension of our Lord. The wooden bridge
over the Rhine at Mayence, which he had
caused to be constructed with admirable skill,
at the cost of ten years' hard work, so that it
seemed as if it might last forever, was so completely consumed in three hours by an acciden- *May, 813*
tal fire that not a single splinter of it was left,
except what was under water. Moreover, one
day in his last campaign into Saxony against *810*
Godfred, King of the Danes, Charles himself
saw a ball of fire fall suddenly from the heav-
ens with a great light, just as he was leaving
camp before sunrise to set out on the march. It
rushed across the clear sky from right to left,
and everybody was wondering what was the
meaning of the sign, when the horse which he
was riding gave a sudden plunge, head fore-
most, and fell, and threw him to the ground so
heavily that his cloak buckle was broken and
his sword belt shattered; and after his servants had hastened to him and relieved him
of his arms, he could not rise without their assistance. He happened to have a javelin in his
hand when he was thrown, and this was struck
from his grasp with such force that it was
found lying at a distance of twenty feet or
more from the spot. Again, the palace at Aix-

la-Chapelle frequently trembled, the roofs of
whatever buildings he tarried in kept up a continual crackling noise, the basilica in which he
was afterwards buried was struck by lightning,
and the gilded ball that adorned the pinnacle
of the roof was shattered by the thunderbolt
and hurled upon the bishop's house adjoining.
In this same basilica, on the margin of the
cornice that ran around the interior, between
the upper and lower tiers of arches, a legend
was inscribed in red letters, stating who was
the builder of the temple, the last words of
which were *Karolus Princeps*. The year that
he died it was remarked by some, a few
months before his decease, that the letters of
the word *Princeps* were so effaced as to be no
longer decipherable. But Charles despised, or
affected to despise, all these omens, as having
no reference whatever to him.

XXXIII. It had been his intention to make a
will, that he might give some share in the inheritance to his daughters and the children of
his concubines; but it was begun too late and
811 could not be finished. Three years before his
death, however, he made a division of his treasures, money, clothes, and other movable
goods in the presence of his friends and servants, and called them to witness it, that their
voices might insure the ratification of the dis-

position thus made. He had a summary drawn up of his wishes regarding this distribution of his property, the terms and text of which are as follows:

"In the name of the Lord God, the Almighty Father, Son, and Holy Ghost. This is the inventory and division dictated by the most glorious and most pious Lord Charles, Emperor Augustus, in the 811th year of the Incarnation of our Lord Jesus Christ, in the 43d year of his reign in France and 37th in Italy, the 11th of his empire, and the 4th Indiction, which considerations of piety and prudence have determined him, and the favor of God enabled him, to make of his treasures and money ascertained this day to be in his treasure chamber. In this division he is especially desirous to provide not only that the largess of alms which Christians usually make of their possessions shall be made for himself in due course and order out of his wealth, but also that his heirs shall be free from all doubt, and know clearly what belongs to them, and be able to share their property by suitable partition without litigation or strife. With this intention and to this end he has first divided all his substance and movable goods ascertained to be in his treasure chamber on the day aforesaid in gold, silver, precious stones, and royal

ornaments into three lots, and has subdivided
and set off two of the said lots into twenty-one
parts, keeping the third entire. The first two
lots have been thus subdivided into twenty-
one parts because there are in his kingdom
twenty-one[83] recognized metropolitan cities,
and in order that each archbishopric may re-
ceive by way of alms, at the hands of his heirs
and friends, one of the said parts, and that the
archbishop who shall then administer its affairs
shall take the part given to it, and share the
same with his suffragans in such manner that
one third shall go to the Church, and the re-
maining two thirds be divided among the suffragans. The twenty-one parts into which the
first two lots are to be distributed, according
to the number of recognized metropolitan
cities, have been set apart one from another,
and each has been put aside by itself in a box
labeled with the name of the city for which it
is destined. The names of the cities to which
this alms or largess is to be sent are as follows:
Rome, Ravenna, Milan, Friuli, Grado,
Cologne, Mayence, Salzburg, Treves, Sens,
Besançon, Lyons, Rouen, Rheims, Arles, Vien-
ne, Moutiers-en-Tarantaise, Embrun, Bor-
deaux, Tours, and Bourges. The third lot,
which he wishes to be kept entire, is to be
bestowed as follows: While the first two lots

are to be divided into the parts aforesaid, and
set aside under seal, the third lot shall be em-
ployed for the owner's daily needs, as property
which he shall be under no obligation to part
with in order to the fulfillment of any vow,
and this as long as he shall be in the flesh, or
consider it necessary for his use. But upon his
death, or voluntary renunciation of the affairs
of this world, this said lot shall be divided into
four parts, and one thereof shall be added to
the aforesaid twenty-one parts; the second
shall be assigned to his sons and daughters,
and to the sons and daughters of his sons, to be
distributed among them in just and equal partition; the third, in accordance with the custom common among Christians, shall be devoted to the poor; and the fourth shall go to
the support of the men servants and maid servants on duty in the palace. It is his wish that
to this said third lot of the whole amount,
which consists, as well as the rest, of gold and
silver, shall be added all the vessels and uten-
sils of brass, iron, and other metals, together
with the arms, clothing, and other movable
goods, costly and cheap, adapted to divers
uses, as hangings, coverlets, carpets, woolen
stuffs, leathern articles, pack-saddles, and
whatsoever shall be found in his treasure
chamber and wardrobe at that time, in order

that thus the parts of the said lot may be aug-
mented, and the alms distributed reach more
persons. He ordains that his chapel—that is
to say, its church property, as well that which
he has provided and collected as that which
came to him by inheritance from his father—
shall remain entire, and not be dissevered by
any partition whatever. If, however, any vessels, books, or other articles be found therein
which are certainly known not to have been
given by him to the said chapel, whoever
wants them shall have them on paying their
value at a fair estimation. He likewise commands that the books which he has collected
in his library in great numbers shall be sold for
fair prices to such as want them, and the
money received therefrom given to the poor.
It is well known that among his other property
and treasures are three silver tables, and one
very large and massive golden one. He directs
and commands that the square silver table,
upon which there is a representation of the city
of Constantinople, shall be sent to the Basilica
of St. Peter the Apostle at Rome, with the
other gifts destined therefor; that the round
one, adorned with a delineation of the city of
Rome, shall be given to the Episcopal Church
at Ravenna; that the third, which far sur-
passes the other two in weight and in beauty

of workmanship, and is made in three circles, showing the plan of the whole universe,[84] drawn with skill and delicacy, shall go, together with the golden table, fourthly above mentioned, to increase that lot which is to be devoted to his heirs and to alms.

This deed, and the dispositions thereof, he has made and appointed in the presence of the bishops, abbots, and counts able to be present, whose names are hereto subscribed: Bishops— Hildebald,[85] Ricolf,[86] Arno,[87] Wolfar,[88] Bernoin,[89] Laidrad,[90] John,[91] Theodulf,[92] Jesse,[93] Heito,[94] Waltgaud.[95] Abbots — Fredugis,[96] Adalung,[97] Angilbert,[98] Irmino.[99] Counts — Walacho,[100] Meginher, Otulf, Stephen, Unruoch, Burchard, Meginhard, Hatto, Rihwin, Edo, Ercangar, Gerold, Bero, Hildiger, Rocculf."

Charles' son Louis, who by the grace of God succeeded him, after examining this summary, *814* took pains to fulfill all its conditions most religiously as soon as possible after his father's death.

NOTES

1. Childeric III, 743–52.
2. Stephen II (or III), 752–57. He anointed Pepin in 754. His predecessor, Zacharias, had ordered the deposition of Childeric just before his death, in 752.
3. The badge of honor and freedom. See Grimm's *Deutsche Rechtsalterthümer*, pp. 146, 239.
4. An ancient royal custom, according to Grimm's *Deutsche Rechtsalterthümer*, p. 262.
5. Not L'Étang de Berre, but a small stream emptying into L'Étang de Sijean.
6. In fact more than sixteen years.
7. See V.
8. This account of the division is somewhat inaccurate.
9. Gerberga.
10. One was named Pepin.
11. In fact more than three years.
12. Charles was born in 742. See XXX and XXXI. The day of his birth is supposed to have been April 2, on the testimony of a ninth-century calendar of the Monastery of Lorsch. The place of his birth is wholly uncertain. See Mabillon's *De Re Diplomaticâ Suppl.* cap. IX.
13. See III.
14. Hadrian I., 772–95.
15. Stephen II (or III), 752–57.

16. At the time of Witikind's great revolt in 782, Charles had 4500 Saxons beheaded in one day at Verden, on the Aller.

17. The Lippescher Wald, a part of the great Teutoburger Wald.

18. Near Osnabrück, at a place called, in the Middle Ages, Schlachtvörderberg, now known as Die Clüs.

19. The Saxon war began in 772; the Italian war in 773.

20. Roncesvalles.

21. This is the only mention in history of this famous character.

22. Liutberga.

23. The Baltic Sea.

24. Modern Esthonia owes its name to the Aïsti.

25. The Huns had aided and abetted Tassilo. See XI.

26. The subject of the verb is not expressed in the original, and this passage is commonly rendered "The Franks had passed," etc., which makes the sentence meaningless.

27. The Tarsatica of olden time, very near Tarsaticum (Fiume).

28. He was brother to Hildegard, Charles' wife.

29. Bohemian war, 805–6; Linonian war, 808.

30. From October 9, 768, to January 28, 814, the date of Charles' death, is little more than forty-five years. The number forty-seven is arrived at by considering the years 768 and 814 as complete.

31. Roman miles.

32. Alfonso II, the Chaste, 791–842.

33. None of them has come down to us.

34. The famous Haroun al Raschid, fifth of the Abassids, 786–809.

35. Nicephorus I, 802–11.

36. Michael I, 811–13.
37. Leo V, 813–20.
38. These palaces were both rebuilt by Frederick Barbarossa. The one at Ingelheim is described at length by Ermoldus Nigellus, *Carm.* iv. 181–282.
39. Her name is variously given; perhaps Desiderata has the best authority. According to the Monk of St. Gall, Charles repudiated her because she was an invalid, and unable to bear children.
40. He was at first called Carloman, but took the name of Pepin when he was baptized and anointed King of Italy by Hadrian I, in 781.
41. He was one of twins. His twin brother, Lothar, died in infancy. See Genealogical Table.
42. Einhard omits Adelaide and Hildegard. See Genealogical Table.
43. See Note 54.
44. See Note 98.
45. She became Abbess of Notre Dame d'Argenteuil, near Paris.
46. She became Abbess of Faremoutiers, according to Father Anselm.
47. She was the daughter of Rodolph, Count of Franconia.
48. Supposed by some to have been Himiltrud, mother of Pepin the Hunchback. See Note 58.
49. Some texts read "four concubines—Mathalgard, who bore him a daughter named Rothild Gersuinda," etc. Those who accept this reading identify Rothild with Rothild, Abbess of Faremoutiers. See the charter published by Mabillon in *Annal. Ord. Bened.* ii. 745, in which the Emperor Lothar styles the latter "our beloved aunt."
50. They both received the tonsure in 818. Drogo became Bishop of Metz, and died December 8, 855.

Hugh became Abbot of St. Quentin, and died June 14, 844.

51. Theodoric, born 810, received the tonsure at the same time with Drogo and Hugh.

52. Charles had three sisters (see Genealogical Table), but Gisela was for many years the only one surviving.

53. At Chelles, near Paris.

54. Constantine VI, 780–802. Marriage did not follow this betrothal. Hruodrud had by Roderick, Count of Maine, a natural son, Louis, who became Abbot of St. Denis, and died in 867.

55. His eyes were put out by order of Louis the Pious, and he died in consequence in 817.

56. He married Bertha to Angilbert. See Note 98.

57. See Note 54 and Note 98.

58. According to Paulus Diaconus, *Gesta Epp. Mett.* *(Mon. Germ. Script.* ii. 265), and other authorities, the name of this concubine was Himiltrud. Pope Stephen II (or III) has been thought to refer to her as Charles' lawful wife, in a letter written by him in 770 to Charles and Carloman. Her son, Pepin, is named before Hildegard's sons in certain litanies compiled shortly after Charles' marriage with Fastrada. She is supposed by some to have been also the mother of Ruodhaid, mentioned in XVIII. Pepin the Hunchback died in 811.

59. Hadrian I, 772–95.

60. Leo III, 795–816.

61. At the capture of Pavia in 774 (see VI), Charles found Peter teaching there, and carried him off to install him in his palace school. No work of his has reached us.

62. Alcuin was born at York in 735, came to Charles' court about 782, and died Abbot of St. Martin of Tours, in 804.

63. See letter of Hadrian I to Charles, in Jaffé's "Monumenta Carolina," p. 268.
64. In 774, 781, 787, and 800.
65. See Note 30.
66. The Salic and Ripuarian.
67. Of the Saxons, Frisians, and Thuringians.
68. Winter month.
69. Horn-shedding (of stags).
70. Spring month.
71. Easter month.
72. Pasture month.
73. Break (ground) month.
74. Hay month.
75. Ears (of grain) month.
76. Wood month.
77. Vintage month.
78. Harvest month.
79. Holy month.
80. The compass, according to Charles, is boxed by twelve points therefore, as follows: N., NE., EN., E., ES., SE., S., SW., WS., W., WN., NW.
81. Admitting the date of Charles' birth to have been April 2, 742 (see Note 12), he was not quite seventy years and ten months old when he died.
82. See Note 30.
83. There were, in fact, twenty-two. Narbonne is omitted from the list for reasons unknown.
84. The Ptolemaic universe, as modified by Aristotle and Hipparchus. The Primum Mobile was added later. For a diagram and brief description of the Ptolemaic universe, see Masson's Introduction to *Paradise Lost* in his edition of Milton's *Poetical Works*.
85. Cologne.
86. Mayence.

87. Salzburg.
88. Rheims.
89. Besançon.
90. Lyons.
91. Arles.
92. Orleans.
93. Amiens.
94. Basle.
95. Liège.
96. St. Bertin in St. Omer. (St. Martin of Tours—Jaffé.)
97. St. Vedast in Arras. (Lorsch.—Jaffé.)
98. Angilbert had been first dean of the Chapter in the palace of Pepin, King of Italy, Duke of Maritime France, and Charles' Prime Minister; but in 790 he retired to the monastery of Centulum in St. Riquier, and became its abbot several years previous to his death, in 814. He was bred at court, and had an intrigue with Charles' daughter Bertha, who had two sons by him—Hartnidus and Nithardus the historian. Charles legitimated this union in 787. Bertha took the veil when Angilbert became a monk. Little except the *Carmen de Karolo Magno* remains to show Angilbert's literary ability.
99. St. Germain in Paris.
100. He was afterward Abbot of Corvey.

GENEALOGICAL TABLE

THE FAMILY OF CHARLES AND HILDEGARD

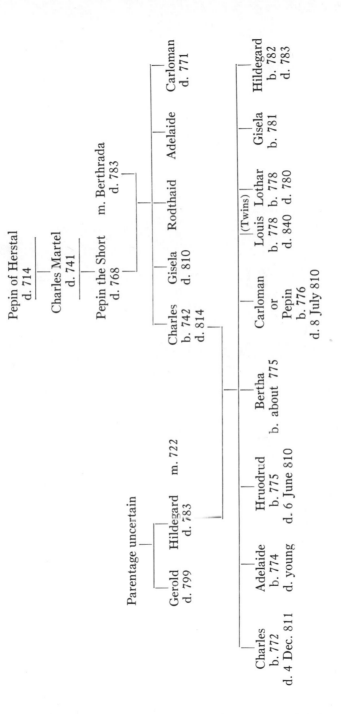

Pepin of Herstal
d. 714

Charles Martel
d. 741

Pepin the Short   m. Berthrada
d. 768   d. 783

Charles   Gisela   Rodthaid   Adelaide   Carloman
b. 742   d. 810   d. 771
d. 814

Parentage uncertain

Gerold   Hildegard   m. 722
d. 799   d. 783

Charles   Adelaide   Hruodrud   Bertha   Carloman   Louis   Lothar   Gisela   Hildegard
b. 772   b. 774   b. 775   b. about 775   or   b. 778   b. 778   b. 781   b. 782
d. 4 Dec. 811   d. young   d. 6 June 810   Pepin   d. 840   d. 780   d. 783
                                                                  b. 776
                                                                  d. 8 July 810

(Twins)

SELECTED ANN ARBOR PAPERBACKS

works of enduring merit

For a complete list of Ann Arbor Paperback titles write:

THE UNIVERSITY OF MICHIGAN PRESS / ANN ARBOR